Profiles in American History

The Life and Times of

SAMUEL ADAMS

Mitchell Lane
PUBLISHERS

P.O. Box 196 · Hockessin, Delaware 19707

Titles in the Series

The Life and Times of

SAMUEL
ADAMS

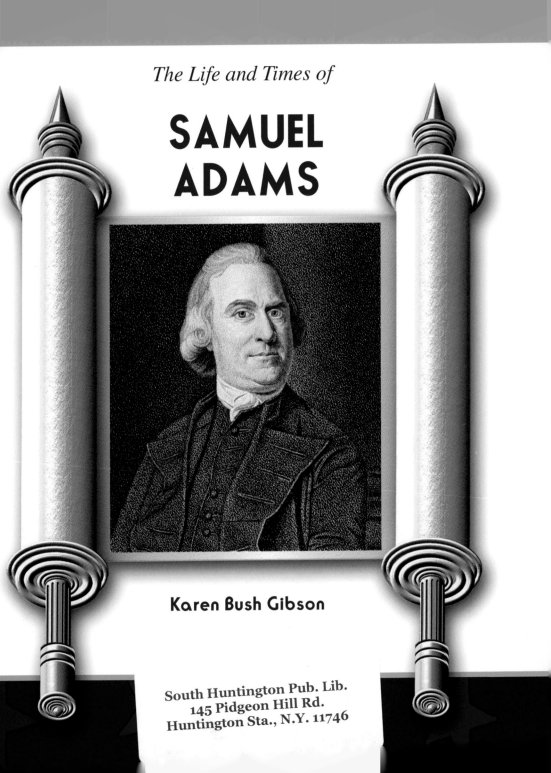

Karen Bush Gibson

Printing   1   2   3   4   5   6   7   8   9

Library of Congress Cataloging-in-Publication Data
Gibson, Karen Bush.
    The life and times of Samuel Adams/Karen Bush Gibson.
        p. cm. — (Profiles in American history)
    Includes bibliographical references and index.
    ISBN 1-58415-440-3 (library bound: alk. paper)
    1. Adams, Samuel, 1722–1803—Juvenile literature. 2. Politicians—United States—Biography—Juvenile literature. 3. United States. Declaration of Independence—Signers—Biography—Juvenile literature. 4. United States—History—Revolution, 1775–1783—Biography—Juvenile literature. I. Title. II. Series.
E302.6 A2G53 2006
973.3092—dc22

                                                     2005036704
ISBN-10: 1-58415-440-3   ISBN-13: 978-1-58415-440-2

ABOUT THE AUTHOR: Karen Bush Gibson considers Samuel Adams a true hero. His selfless actions put others and his country's needs before his own. Writing extensively for the juvenile educational market, Karen's work has included biographies, current events, and cultural histories. More than thirty books for children include *The Life and Times of Catherine the Great, The Fury of Hurricane Andrew, The Life and Times of Eli Whitney,* and *Peter Zenger* for Mitchell Lane Publishers.

PHOTO CREDITS: Cover, pp. 1, 3: Library of Congress; p. 6: Getty Images; pp. 9, 12, 15: Library of Congress; p. 17: North Wind Picture Archives; p. 20: Corbis; pp. 23, 25: Library of Congress; pp. 28, 31: Corbis; p. 34: Library of Congress; p. 37: Corbis; p. 39: Getty Images; p. 40 Library of Congress

Contents

A leading patriot from Boston, Samuel
Adams was one of the earliest opponents
to British taxation of the colonies. He
organized many protests against the
British, including the Boston Tea Party.
Adams advocated that the colonies be
independent from Britain.

CHAPTER 1

A Tea Party

The colonists were angry. How dare the British demand a tax on their tea? The Tea Act, passed by the British Parliament in May 1773—without any input from the colonists—was just another attempt to show the people of America that they were indeed a British colony and subject to British rules and regulations.

The Tea Act was proposed by Lord North in Britain as a way to save Britain's East India Company trade group from failure. The British had gone into debt financing the French and Indian War in America. What better way to make the colonists pay than with a tax?

Samuel Adams, a leading voice in Boston politics, was feeling smug. For years, he had warned his fellow colonists of the dangers of their situation with Britain. Now maybe they would listen. The only solution, he felt, was declaring America an independent country.

The *Dartmouth,* a ship bringing tea from Britain, arrived Sunday, November 28. Although the colonists usually did not meet for business on Sundays, this time they made an exception. After the meeting, men posted notices all over town to summon the colonists to gather the next morning.

FRIENDS!   BRETHREN!   COUNTRYMEN!
That worst of all plagues, the detestable tea…is now arrived
in this harbour, the hour of destruction or manly opposition
to the machinations of tyranny stares you in the face.[1]

On Monday, people crowded into Faneuil Hall at 9:00 A.M. Adams organized them for action. The people of Boston demanded that the agents in charge of collecting the tea taxes send the ships back to England. The tea agents refused. No doubt they were more frightened of British soldiers than of a few rabble-rousers. Twenty-five men took turns watching the harbor from Griffin's Wharf to make certain the tea stayed on board. Meanwhile, two more ships arrived.

Samuel Adams sent letters to neighboring towns, encouraging action. He had long believed that the most effective means of communication was a network between the colonies. He talked to people in the streets. He spent many hours speaking to people in the Green Dragon Tavern. Did they understand what King George was trying to do? This time it was a tea tax. Next time it would be a tax on something else. The British would tax them to death, and they didn't even get a say in it. According to Adams, the Tea Act "would destroy the colonial economy and also support Britain's claim that Parliament could bind the colonials in all cases whatsoever."[2]

As the cold air whipped around one wintry evening, the colonists met one last time. It was December 16, 1773, the day of decision. Nearly every adult in Boston crowded into the forty-four-year-old Old South Meeting House, the largest building in Boston. Two thousand more from the outer villages joined them. Speeches and jokes were bantered about while they awaited an answer from the governor. The colonists had issued a demand to Governor Hutchinson that he send the three tea ships away once and for all.

The front door opened, and the messenger entered with the governor's answer: No. The governor would not send the ships back to England. The crowd grew quiet. The mood had turned serious . . . and angry. Adams stood up and looked at the many faces, then said, "This meeting can do nothing more to save the country!"[3]

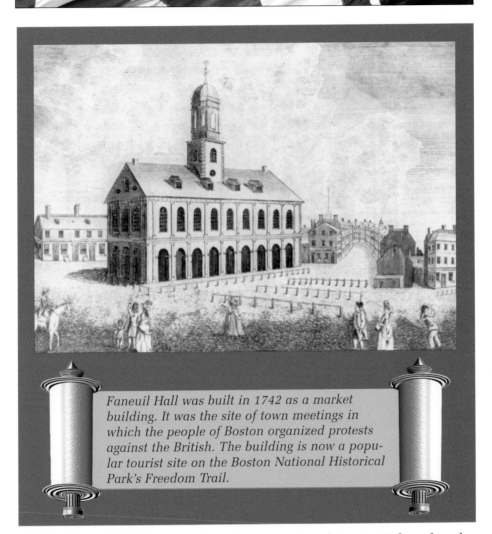

Faneuil Hall was built in 1742 as a market building. It was the site of town meetings in which the people of Boston organized protests against the British. The building is now a popular tourist site on the Boston National Historical Park's Freedom Trail.

To the Loyalists, people who were loyal to British rule, the words probably meant nothing. But many believe Adams's words were a signal. Forty or fifty men, dressed as Mohawk Indians, stood just inside the entrance. These "Indians" were actually colonists who had agreed to dump the tea in the harbor. The disguises were meant to hide their real identities from the British, but two men were recognizable: Dr. Joseph Warren and a silversmith named Paul Revere. At Adams's words, the "Mohawks," with hatchets in their hands, moved down Milk Street to Griffin's Wharf in Boston Harbor. A mob of at least a hundred people trailed them, with

only lanterns and torches to light their way on the moonless night. Maybe a thousand others watched and cheered them on, including John Hancock, who was heard to say, "Let every man do what is right in his own eyes!"

Where was Samuel Adams during one of the most important events of American history? "Friend and foe alike testified that Samuel Adams was the leading light in Boston's fight against the Tea Act,"[4] wrote John K. Alexander, author of *Samuel Adams: America's Revolutionary Politician.* Throughout his life, Adams never kept letters for their historical value, nor did he feel compelled to write an autobiography or keep a journal. He also wasn't one to take any credit. By his reasoning, it was the good people of Boston who decided their course of action. Much of what we know about Adams was written by others.

At fifty-one years of age, Samuel Adams was already an "old man" in an era when many died in their fifties. As the crowd moved to the harbor, he reportedly stayed behind in the meeting house. Although he didn't physically participate in the Boston Tea Party, surely he watched as the "Mohawks" boarded the *Dartmouth, Eleanor,* and *Beaver.*

With hatchets raised, the men smashed open 342 chests filled with tea. They picked up the chests and dumped 90,000 pounds of tea overboard, into the harbor.

The next day, Adams wrote about the success of the Boston Tea Party. Paul Revere rushed the information to other towns, reaching Philadelphia the day after Christmas. Other harbor towns, including New York City and Annapolis, Maryland, had their own tea parties the next year. Inspired by the Boston Tea Party, the rest of the colonies refused to implement the tea tax. It was time for a Revolution!

Boston

Boston, one of America's oldest cities, was established in 1630 by Puritans. It soon became the political and cultural center of New England, plus the capital of Massachusetts Bay Colony. Located on a peninsula between the Charles River and Boston Harbor, the land

A Modern Photograph of Boston

was once the home of Massachusett Indians, most of whom died from measles and scarlet fever, diseases brought by the Europeans.

Boston began as a village of Puritan craftspeople, farmers, and ministers who had been persecuted in England for their religious beliefs. By the eighteenth century, Boston was a thriving town and a leading commercial, fishing, and shipbuilding center for the colonies. More importantly, it became the center of the struggle for independence from Britain. It is noted as the site of the Boston Massacre and the Boston Tea Party. Three of the major battles of the American Revolution took place not far from Boston in 1775. In March 1776, General George Washington ordered his troops to occupy Dorchester Heights, overlooking Boston. Washington's troops threatened to fire cannons at the British troops guarding Boston. The British fled the town, and the first major American victory of the revolution was won.

When the war ended, Boston became one of the world's busiest ports for foreign trade. It was chartered as a city in 1822. Landfill projects provided more land for the city to grow. In the 1840s, more than half a million Irish immigrants escaped starvation from Ireland's potato famine by moving to Boston. The city became a popular center for the abolitionist movement. Harriet Beecher Stowe's antislavery novel, *Uncle Tom's Cabin,* was published in Boston.

By 2006, Boston was home to about 590,000 residents and many universities and colleges. Millions of travelers visit Boston each year for its rich history. Many famous colonial buildings, including Old North Church, King's Chapel, and Faneuil Hall, still stand.

For Your Information

Colonial Boston was a busy seaport that centered around the harbor. Homes and stores were close to Boston Harbor. Merchants and townspeople eagerly awaited the news and supplies from England when a ship came to port.

CHAPTER 2

Politics

A baby boy was born to Samuel and Mary Adams on September 27, 1722, in Boston, Massachusetts. On the very same day at the New South Church on Summer Street, the baby was christened Samuel Adams. Like many boys of the day, he was named after his father.

Samuel was the fourth of twelve children born to his parents; only three of the children would survive to adulthood. This survival rate was common during this time period. Immunizations and antibiotics had not been invented yet, and babies were often too weak to fight illness. In addition to Samuel, there was his older sister, Mary, and a younger brother, Joseph.

Although Samuel's father worked as a brewer, he was best known as Deacon Adams. Besides serving as a deacon at the New South Church, he also held other offices—justice of the peace, town official, and state representative. He was a successful and widely respected man in Boston.

The Adams family lived in a large house next to the father's brewery. The house sat on a large parcel of land that extended from Purchase Street to Boston Harbor. It included a garden and an orchard. Perhaps Samuel most enjoyed the rooftop observatory that gave him a view of the harbor.

As a child, Samuel Adams had the freedom to wander all over the busy seaport town of Boston. According to historian David Hackett Fischer, "No part of the town was more than a few blocks from salt water. The housefronts echoed to the cry of oystermen."[1] Samuel learned at a young age that there were wealthy people in Boston. He also knew that some people were quite poor. He liked to listen to people talk about issues and problems. Perhaps Deacon Adams noticed this about his son. Regardless, he was determined that his son would have a better education than he had.

The Adamses enrolled Samuel in the Boston Latin School at the age of seven. Established in 1635, Boston Latin was the first public school in colonial America. Classes started at seven o'clock (eight o'clock in winter) and lasted until five in the afternoon. Students had a two-hour break from 11:00 A.M. to 1:00 P.M. Samuel learned to read and write and do math. Boston Latin School also focused heavily on Latin and Greek classics. Students were expected to memorize passages in Latin and recite them.

When he was almost fourteen, Samuel graduated from Boston Latin School, and his thoughts turned to college. The oldest and one of the most illustrious colleges was Harvard, a short walk for the teenager across a bridge over the Charles River. Even though his parents' home was in Boston, he lived on the hundred-year-old campus, as did all students. He stayed with his parents four days each month, plus during a six-week summer break.

Morning classes started at six o'clock. The early afternoon hours were spent in recreational activities, followed by studying. Samuel studied theology, Greek, and Latin. He also discovered the works of seventeenth-century English philosopher John Locke, whose essays influenced politics. In his *Second Treatise on Civil Government,* Locke introduces the idea of government as a social agreement between people. He mentions the ideas of "a separation of legislative, executive, and federative (or foreign affairs) powers."[2] By the early eighteenth century, the idea of separation of powers was much discussed in British government, and it appealed to Samuel's political mind.

Samuel received a bachelor's degree at age seventeen, but he still didn't know what he wanted to do with his life. His parents let him continue at Harvard to work on a graduate degree. Although well

John Locke (1632–1704) was a British philosopher who wrote about religion and politics. His writings influenced American colonists. The British considered Locke a revolutionary: His ideas defended the British uprising known as the Glorious Revolution of 1688.

liked by other students, Samuel didn't always fit in. He didn't care much about sports or making a good impression with his appearance. He often wore the same suit until it was in tatters. He preferred to spend his time talking to people about politics. He could often be found in a nearby tavern—taverns were the informal meeting places of the time—debating some issue of government.

Adams graduated from Harvard in July 1743 with a master's degree. The normally dull graduation services were livened up when Adams began to speak about why resisting an unjust government was a good idea. Governor Jonathan Belcher, who attended the festivities, took notice.

By this time, Adams was twenty years old. Most men his age entered a profession, but Adams didn't know what he was supposed to do with his life. Because Samuel enjoyed speaking so much, his father had hoped he might be a lawyer. In the eighteenth century, a person became a lawyer by studying and learning from an experienced lawyer. Afterward, the student had to pass a test. Adams began his legal studies, but quit before he got very far. It is not clear why he stopped, but it was reported that his mother didn't think

much of lawyers. The Adamses were Puritans, and Mary Adams was a very religious woman who hoped her son might be a minister. Although Samuel shared his mother's Puritan beliefs, he had no desire to be a minister.

A friend of Samuel's father, Thomas Cushing Sr., hired Samuel to work in his counting house, which was similar to a modern bank. Samuel worked as a clerk, spending his day adding and subtracting in ledgers. The only part of his day that he enjoyed seemed to be when he broke for mealtime at noon. He often spent this time in taverns discussing politics. Before long, Samuel lost his job.

Samuel's family had suffered financial problems while he was in college. His father and some friends had founded Land Bank Company, a private bank. They used their homes as security. Unhappy with the competition, rich merchants convinced officials to force Land Bank out of business. Samuel's father owed a lot of money. Officials tried to take the house on Purchase Street, but so far father and son had been able to fight them off. The only other thing of value that Samuel's father owned was the brewery. With other resources exhausted, he hired Samuel to work at the brewery. It is unclear how much responsibility the young man had. He had proven over and over that he had little regard for money. He was just as likely to give it away when he had it.

Historian John K. Alexander, who calls Adams the first professional and modern politician, said that Adams was a failure as a businessman. The only business he seemed to care about was politics. In late 1747, Adams took this interest in politics and joined some friends in a club that lashed out at the government. Beginning in January 1848, they published a newspaper, the *Public* (or *Independent*) *Advertiser*. According to Adams, the purpose of the *Public Advertiser* was to defend the rights of the working people. No doubt this is where Adams learned to write persuasively.

The newspaper published political essays by Adams and his friends. In one essay that might have been written by Adams, the *Advertiser* reported, "The true Object of Loyalty is a good Legal Constitution that [allows] a student to remonstrate his Grievances."[3]

A few months after the publication of the first *Advertiser*, Samuel Adams's father died. He was fifty-eight. The *Advertiser* called

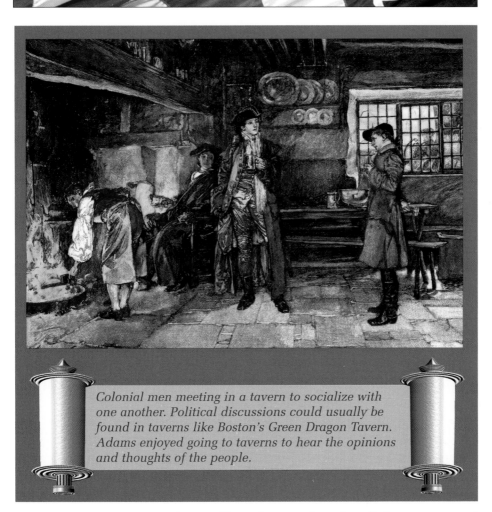

Colonial men meeting in a tavern to socialize with one another. Political discussions could usually be found in taverns like Boston's Green Dragon Tavern. Adams enjoyed going to taverns to hear the opinions and thoughts of the people.

Deacon Adams "one who well understood and rightly persevered the Civil and Religious Interests of these People [of Boston]—a true New-England Man—A Honest Patriot."[4]

Within a year of his father's death, his mother also died. With the responsibility of making funeral arrangements, Adams spent a lot of time in the household of the Reverend Checkley. The reverend had long been the Adamses pastor and was even the one who had christened Samuel. Samuel noticed the reverend's daughter Elizabeth and began courting her.

On October 17, 1749, Samuel Adams and Elizabeth Checkley were married. The Reverend Checkley conducted the wedding

ceremony. The Adamses moved into Samuel's childhood home on Purchase Street. They had six children in eight years. Only one son (Samuel) and one daughter (Hannah) lived to adulthood.

Soon after Adams's marriage, the *Independent Advertiser* folded. Adams kept busy with politics and was a regular presence at Boston's town meetings. In 1753, he was chosen for a committee that evaluated schools. Three years later, he was elected to be property tax collector. His job was to collect taxes owed, and he would receive five percent of what he gathered. Adams felt sorry for the people who owed taxes, so he was rarely successful in his job. Meanwhile, Elizabeth delivered their sixth child, a son, who was stillborn. Unable to recover her strength, she died three weeks later. Their son Samuel was five. Hannah was only a year and a half.

Adams struggled with his grief and the trials of raising two children. About a year after Elizabeth's death, he happened to see a notice in the *Boston News-Letter.* His home was to be sold at a public auction the following day. Somehow he was able to delay the auction. Lieutenant Governor Thomas Hutchinson reported that Adams threatened the sheriff. It is uncertain whether Adams did this or not, but he did write a letter to the *Boston News-Letter* promising to sue anyone who held such an auction.

After seven years as a single father, Samuel remarried on December 6, 1764, to Elizabeth Wells, the daughter of a friend of his father's. Reverend Checkley again performed the ceremony. Because his new wife shared the same name as his first wife, he chose to call her Betsy.

Within a few years of marrying, Samuel Adams had to close the already foundering brewery for good. He quit his job as tax collector, which he was never good at in the first place. Adams spent most of his time talking with people about the problems they were experiencing under British rule. He wrote letters, speeches, and papers about the need for independence. He didn't have time for a "real" job, because his job was politics. Yet Adams was a husband and father without a decent income and in danger of losing his home. His cousin, John Adams, who was also active in politics, said in late 1765: "Samuel's only real flaw was probably that he is too attentive to the Public and not enough so to himself and his family."[5]

Harvard

Harvard University is the oldest college in the United States. It's even older than the United States. Established in 1636, Harvard started with nine students. In 2006, Harvard had more than 18,000 regular students and thousands

Harvard

more in special non-degree programs. It is considered one of the ivy league schools. Ivy league schools are very prestigious and include eight old and prominent universities in the northeastern United States.

Harvard was first founded in Newtowne on October 28, 1636. Newtowne was renamed Cambridge in 1638 after Cambridge University in England. It was in 1639 that the school was named Harvard College after its first benefactor, John Harvard, a minister who left his library of over 400 books and half his estate to the school. The Charter of 1650 established a seven-member corporation (the oldest corporation in America) to oversee the college that continues to this day. Harvard offered an education of the classics consistent with the Puritan philosophy of the Pilgrims. Many early graduates became ministers. Until 1708, Harvard's presidents were all ministers.

During the American Revolution, Harvard fed American soldiers. After George Washington's Continental Army forced the British to leave Boston, Harvard gave Washington an honorary degree.

As the college grew, it focused more on a broader curriculum favoring intellectual independence. The poet Henry Wadsworth Longfellow was one of many students who enjoyed the enlightened classes. His daughter, Alice Mary, became one of the first female students in 1878—about the time that the college progressed to a university.

Harvard has a reputation for producing graduates who excel in their chosen professions. Harvard's graduates include seven presidents: John Adams, John Quincy Adams, Theodore Roosevelt, Franklin Delano Roosevelt, Rutherford B. Hayes, John Fitzgerald Kennedy, and George W. Bush.

King George III succeeded his grandfather, George II, in 1760, and served for sixty years. He opposed American independence, but it was Parliament that was responsible for most of the policies that the colonists rebelled against.

CHAPTER 3

"Liberty, Property, and No Stamps!"

By 1765, King George III of England had heard about this revolutionary named Samuel Adams, but he had other things to worry about. When Britain defeated the French in the French and Indian War, England gained control of many French and Spanish possessions in America. It also left the king with a huge debt. British politicians in Parliament decided that people in England were already heavily taxed, and that the burden of the debt should fall to the colonists.

Parliament passed the Stamp Act on March 22, 1765, as the first major tax on the colonists. Effective November 1, the legislation directed the colonists to buy special stamps that would be used on newspapers, wills, and all kinds of other documents.

Colonists were outraged at being charged to help the British pay for the French and Indian War. Nowhere was the disagreement louder than in Boston. Samuel Adams talked to merchants, dockworkers, farmers, and blacksmiths. He spoke to young and old. He knew that if defiance led to battle, it would be the young men who'd fight the battles. He wrote letters to newspapers throughout the colonies, attacking the Stamp Act. He stirred people up at town meetings. He began rallying men together to fight for the colonists' rights. To his surprise, the colonists even had allies in Britain—people who also opposed the Stamp Act.

"No taxation without representation" was on everyone's lips. How was it fair for the British to tax them when the colonists weren't even allowed to vote in England?

Adams focused on legal ways of opposing the Stamp Act—boycotting British goods and staging large nonviolent demonstrations. The first group to protest the Stamp Act did so on August 14, 1765. The growing crowd began to shout, "Liberty, property, and no stamps!" They forced tax stamp distributor Andrew Oliver, brother-in-law to Lieutenant Governor Thomas Hutchinson, to resign by wrecking his home. They hung the tax collector in effigy from a giant elm where Orange, Newbury, and Essex Streets met. The large, unruly crowd had no apparent leader. Authorities could find no one to arrest, although Hutchinson strongly suspected Samuel Adams was the instigator of the rebellious group. Hutchinson was a strict Loyalist who had been part of the Land Bank problems that the senior Samuel Adams had experienced. Hutchinson and the younger Adams would butt heads over and over again.

A group of shopkeepers and craftsmen formed the Loyal Nine, the first organized group dedicated to the rights of colonists. The Loyal Nine later became the core of the Sons of Liberty. This group received their name from a British lawmaker who opposed the Stamp Act. Colonel Isaac Barré predicted the "sons of liberty" would fight the tax. In Boston alone, three hundred men belonged to the Sons of Liberty. They met regularly at the same elm on which they had hung Oliver's likeness. The tree became known as the Liberty Tree. The idea of the Sons of Liberty spread to other towns, too.

Adams didn't neglect the rich colonists. He courted one of the richest men in town to help with the cause. Adams had little in common with John Hancock, the wealthy merchant who lived at the top of Beacon Hill, but he believed that Hancock could benefit the cause. Adams convinced Hancock to join the Sons of Liberty, thus bringing more attention to this group of American Patriots.

Adams encouraged other men also. Foremost was Dr. Joseph Warren. With his ability to create ornate phrases, Warren soon became as well known a Patriot as another young man, Paul Revere.

Joseph Warren was a physician and good friend to Samuel Adams. A gifted speaker, Dr. Warren often spoke at political gatherings advocating colonial independence. He served in the Provincial Congress of 1774. He volunteered at the Battle of Bunker Hill, where he was killed.

Another important alliance was with area Native American tribes. Adams chaired a committee whose goal was to establish a good relationship with the Six Nations. The Six Nations were six tribes (Cayuga, Mohawk, Oneida, Onondaga, Seneca, and Tuscarora) that had formed a powerful federation soon after the Europeans came to America. They were also known as the Iroquois.

When the Boston representative for the Massachusetts House of Representatives died, Samuel Adams ran for his seat and won on September 27, 1765. He decided that the House would be a good place from which to fight the Stamp Act. He made speeches, appealing to the logic of those around him. Adams continued writing anonymous protests against the Stamp Act to the colonial newspapers. As a representative of the colonial government, he also began writing papers against the Stamp Act for the House of Representatives.

In his biography on Samuel Adams, James K. Alexander wrote about Adams's influence upon the Massachusetts House of Representatives. Soon, the Congress was warning Britain that the proposed Stamp Act would affect American purchases of British goods, saying, "thus for both Constitutional and pragmatic reasons, Parliament should repeal the Stamp Act and other recent laws restricting American commerce."[1]

Adams worked tirelessly for the cause of repealing the Stamp Act. He often rose before others and stayed awake writing one of his many letters long after others went to bed. He realized that the Bostonians' dissent would be more powerful if they joined with people from other towns and colonies. He began writing to Patriots in all thirteen colonies.

On the day the Stamp Act was to take effect, the colonists in Boston hung more effigies from the Liberty Tree. The next day, the figures were cut down and taken to the public gallows. Meanwhile, there was no one to implement the Stamp Act. All the stamp tax agents had resigned. The situation was similar throughout the colonies. However, Adams didn't feel as if they had won any victory until a ship came into port on May 16, 1766, with the news that Parliament had repealed the Stamp Act.

With the Stamp Act repealed, the colonists rejoiced and returned to their everyday lives. Unlike Adams, most of the rebels had jobs and interests outside of politics. Soon after the repeal of the Stamp Act, Adams noticed that Parliament had passed another law. The Declaratory Act stated that Parliament had the right to make laws for the thirteen colonies in all cases. Few of the colonists seemed concerned about the Declaratory Act. It said nothing about taxes. Many believed that this was just England's way of showing them who was boss. Adams knew it was only a matter of time before Britain forced another tax on them.

He was right. The next set of taxes came from the Townshend Acts, named after the British treasurer, Charles Townshend. Townshend said that the Americans needed to recognize the authority of Parliament. The Townshend Acts allowed the taxing of paint, paper, tea, lead, and glass. Additionally, Britain promised to enforce the Navigation Acts, which prohibited the colonists from trading with other countries.

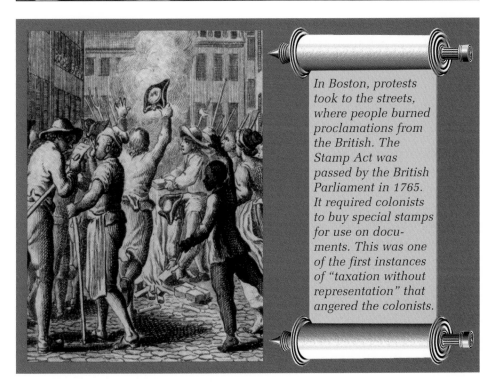

In Boston, protests took to the streets, where people burned proclamations from the British. The Stamp Act was passed by the British Parliament in 1765. It required colonists to buy special stamps for use on documents. This was one of the first instances of "taxation without representation" that angered the colonists.

Adams once again began writing letters and talking to people. He convinced both Boston and the colony of Massachusetts to boycott British goods. Soon, other colonies followed their example.

Meanwhile, one of Hancock's ships was confiscated. Britain first saw the colonies as a moneymaking proposition. It wanted to control all the importing and exporting of items, sometimes charging very high fees for goods. Smuggling became a way that Americans could obtain the goods they needed without paying the high fees. Part of Hancock's uncle's business had been the importing and exporting of goods by ship. Like many others, he tried to do this free of British rules and regulations. Hancock had continued his uncle's practice of smuggling. When the *Liberty* arrived in the harbor with more than a hundred casks of wine from Portugal, British customs officials confiscated it. This event angered the Bostonians in a way that news of the Townshend Acts hadn't. They threw bricks at the customs agents and even took one of their boats and burned it.

On October 1, 1768, seven hundred British soldiers marched into Boston with muskets on their shoulders to restore order to Boston.

More troops continued to arrive until there was approximately one soldier for every man in town. Skirmishes were reported with regularity. Things were getting worse for the colonists. They no longer doubted Samuel Adams. Tempers flared at the sight of the British soldiers.

On March 5, 1770, a group of men and boys shouted insults and threw snowballs at soldiers outside the barracks on King Street. Confusion followed and the British soldiers killed five people, one of them a seventeen-year-old boy. Adams named it the "Boston Massacre." Silversmith Paul Revere created an engraving commemorating the event.

Immediately after the Boston Massacre, Bostonians demanded that the soldiers leave Boston. Hutchinson told the colonists that he didn't have the authority to remove the troops. The crowds grew to thousands, all demanding that the soldiers leave. Fearful of what might happen, the troops were ordered to leave Boston—all except for the soldiers who had shot their weapons. They stood trial. Samuel Adams insisted that the men receive a fair trial. John Adams represented them, and all but two were acquitted. The two who were found guilty were given light sentences. Both Adams cousins wanted the British to know that the colonists intended to be fair.

With the colonists boycotting British goods, the Townshend Acts failed. All the taxes were repealed except for the one on tea. Most Americans felt that this was a victory, but Samuel Adams insisted that one tax was just as bad as many. There were enough colonists who agreed with them. The Boston Tea Party of 1773 was the strongest rebellion the British had witnessed. Secretly, Adams had been happy about the Tea Act. According to him, "the British government could not have devised a more effectual Measure to unite the Colonies."[2]

As the British struggled with how to punish the instigators of the Boston Tea Party, Adams moved ahead with a meeting at the Old South Meeting House. John Hancock was very popular with the people, so Adams chose him to give the speech proposing an independent country, America. Samuel Adams wrote letters proposing independence and sent riders to deliver them throughout the colonies.

John Hancock

John Hancock (1737–1793) was born in Braintree (now Quincy), Massachusetts. His minister father died when he was a boy, and John was sent to live with his rich, childless uncle, Thomas Hancock, in Boston. After John graduated from Harvard College in 1754, he joined his uncle's business as a clerk. He was a capable businessman and inherited the company after his uncle's

John Hancock

death. He was said to be one of the richest men in the colonies.

Samuel Adams convinced Hancock to work for colonists' rights. Soon, both were leading revolutionaries in the fight for independence. Hancock used his wealth and influence to aid the colonists' cause. Although Hancock was said to love public attention, he also demonstrated that he was confident in the abilities of the common man.

In 1769, Hancock was elected to the Massachusetts colonial legislature, which in 1774 became the Massachusetts Provincial Congress. He served as president in 1774 and 1775. He also served as president of the Continental Congress from 1775 to 1777. As president, he was the first to sign the Declaration of Independence adopted by the Congress. His signature is large and showy. After signing the Declaration, Hancock, who already had a bounty on his head, commented, "The British ministry can read that name without spectacles; let them double their reward."[3] Since that time, putting your *John Hancock* on something has come to mean "signing your name."

John Hancock had hoped to command the Continental Army, but Congress chose George Washington instead. After the Revolutionary War, Hancock served on the committee that wrote the state constitution for Massachusetts. He became the first governor of the state of Massachusetts under the new United States of America and was repeatedly reelected until his death in 1793.

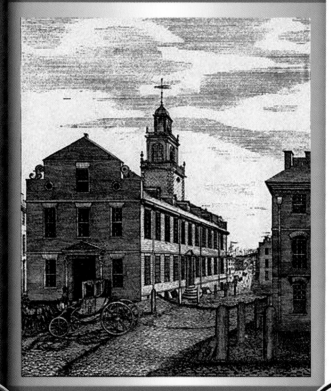

Built in 1713, the Old State House is the oldest surviving public building in Boston. It was built to accommodate the Massachusetts Bay Colony government. The Massachusetts Provincial Congress, of which Samuel Adams was a member, met there.

CHAPTER 4

The Continental Congress

General Thomas Gage, leader of the British troops in the colonies, arrived in Boston to assume the post of governor of Massachusetts. Five thousand soldiers followed. The Patriots worried about John Hancock's and Samuel Adams's safety. But Adams wasn't worried. He continued to walk the streets of Boston and talk with the people as he had done since childhood. Sometimes he even brought his cousin's son, seven-year-old John Quincy Adams.

The British closed Boston Harbor on June 1, 1774. They hoped to force the rebellious colonists into submission by starving them. They didn't realize the other colonies were keeping an eye on Boston. New York, Maryland, Rhode Island, and other colonies shipped food to nearby Massachusetts ports in Salem and Marblehead. From there, the food was secretly taken to the Bostonians. Adams was the chairman of the donations committee in charge of passing out food.

Adams had been thinking for a long time about a congress with representatives from all thirteen colonies. Benjamin Franklin of Philadelphia had also talked of this idea. With the British pressuring the colonies to obey, now seemed like a good time to initiate the plan. The First Continental Congress was scheduled to meet in September 1774 in Philadelphia.

The Massachusetts House of Representatives met on June 17 to vote on their representatives for the Continental Congress. News about the meeting reached Governor Gage, who tried to stop the vote. The legislators ignored him and chose their delegates. Thomas Cushing Jr., James Bowdoin, Robert Treat Paine, John Adams, and Samuel Adams would attend the Continental Congress as representatives of Massachusetts.

Each of the colonies except Georgia sent delegates to the congress, which started on September 5. During their six-week session, the delegates agreed to oppose the British and to boycott British imports. They also adopted a Declaration of Rights and Grievances, which outlined the rights of the people and colonies. They adjourned, agreeing to call another congress if Parliament and King George did not address their issues in a satisfactory manner.

The names of Samuel Adams and John Hancock were often mentioned in association with any trouble in the colonies. Massachusetts, particularly Boston, had proven to be most rebellious. King George had reached the end of his rope. He declared that Massachusetts was openly rebelling against Britain and in early 1775 ordered the arrest of leaders like Samuel Adams and John Hancock.

On April 16, General Gage ordered troops to Concord, where the colonists' military supplies were reportedly kept. Additionally, General Gage may have heard that Adams and Hancock were nearby. They had stopped there on their way to Philadelphia. It would work well for him if he could capture the two infamous Patriots.

Joseph Warren learned of Gage's plans and sent couriers to warn the people of Concord. Late on April 18, Paul Revere was summoned to warn Adams and Hancock of the approach of British troops intent on arresting them. He crossed the Charles River and borrowed a horse. The local Sons of Liberty had seen his signal in the steeple of Boston's Old North Church. Revere's friends had hung two lanterns to indicate that the British were coming by water. If they had hung one lantern, it would have meant the British were traveling over land. Revere shouted as he rode through the countryside. "The British are coming! The redcoats are coming!" Around midnight, he reached the house where Adams and Hancock were staying.

In the morning hours, as Adams and Hancock were moved to another safe house, they likely heard the sounds of shots in the

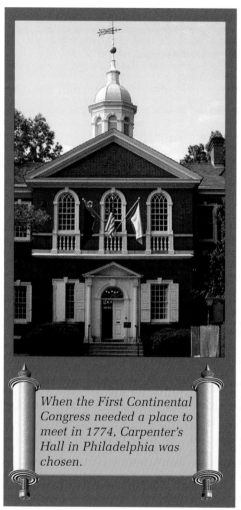

When the First Continental Congress needed a place to meet in 1774, Carpenter's Hall in Philadelphia was chosen.

countryside around Lexington and Concord. The first shots of the American Revolution had been fired. A flag painted with a picture of the Liberty Tree was reportedly carried into battle. Adams was delighted. He reported the battle to newspapers using one of his many pen names. He wrote that America was a country "fighting The Rebel Army. The Americans were fighting the Mercenary Soldiers of a Tyrant."[1]

Bells were often used in the eighteenth century to alert people to news or trouble. In Philadelphia, the bells sounded long and hard. According to Fischer, "the great bell rang a tocsin for the dark news from Lexington and Concord. More than eight thousand people hurried to the State House yard and agreed unanimously (even some Quakers among them) to take up arms in defense of life, liberty, and property."[2]

Weeks after the battle of Lexington, the Second Continental Congress gathered. Parliament had rejected the Declaration sent by the First Continental Congress, and clashes between the colonists and British soldiers were becoming more frequent. It was apparent that independence was the only way for colonists to have any rights. In June, General Gage said that any Americans who laid down their arms would be pardoned, with the exception of Adams and Hancock. They were seen as too dangerous to pardon.

Adams's son, Samuel Adams Jr., was now Dr. Samuel Adams. He had studied medicine under the Dr. Joseph Warren. When Warren

became general of the Massachusetts troops, Adams asked for a medical appointment for his son if he was deserving. So far, Adams had received good reports about his son's work.

Meanwhile, Adams watched men going off to fight. Some didn't come back, including Warren, who was killed at Bunker Hill. Adams wrote to his wife that Dr. Warren "fell in the glorious struggle for the publick Liberty."[3]

The Second Continental Congress established a colonial militia and elected George Washington from Virginia to head it. The delegates drafted a Declaration of Independence, written by delegate Thomas Jefferson. The first signature affixed to the document on July 4, 1776, belonged to John Hancock. The Congress took a brief break in August due to the heat. John Adams convinced his cousin Samuel to ride a horse for the quickest way home and back. Samuel Adams had hardly if ever ridden a horse, but he made the three-hundred-mile trip without problems. When the delegates returned, they continued work on the Articles of Confederation and getting signatures for the Declaration of Independence. The Second Continental Congress adjourned when the last signature was obtained on December 12.

The Third Continental Congress convened eight days later to finish work on the Articles of Confederation, a blueprint to describe how the federal government of the new country would work. Almost a year later, the Articles were finalized and presented to the colonies. The Articles stated that the United States was a Confederation. This meant that each state was essentially its own nation, but the states would join together when necessary, such as in common defense. It took three and a half years—until March 1, 1781—for all the colonies to ratify the Articles of Confederation. Adams wrapped up affairs with the Continental Congress on April 19, 1781, the sixth anniversary of the battle of Lexington, and headed home.

The Revolutionary War officially ended about two years later. A preliminary peace treaty was recognized on November 30, 1782. Britain formally recognized the United States of America as an independent country in the Treaty of Paris, which was signed on September 3, 1783.

It was time to create a government for the new country.

Paul Revere's Ride

Paul Revere

The story of Paul Revere's ride to warn the countryside that the British were coming is now a legend. In truth, Paul Revere was one of many express riders who carried news and messages to other colonies in 1774 and 1775. On the evening of April 18, 1775, Dr. Joseph Warren sent for Revere. News had reached the Patriots that British troops would be leaving Boston and marching to Concord.

According to Revere, "About 10 o'Clock, Dr. Warren Sent in great haste for me, and beged that I would imediately Set off for Lexington, where Messrs. Hancock and Adams were, and acquaint them of the Movement, and that it was thought they were the objets."[4]

Revere rowed across the Charles River, where some men were waiting with a fast horse. On the way to Lexington to warn Samuel Adams and John Hancock of their impending arrest, Revere alerted the countryside. One person in each village would awaken the others, who would assemble and start marching toward Lexington and Concord. Revere was able to warn Adams and Hancock before being joined by another rider, William Dawes. The two decided to continue on to Concord, where the colonial weapons were housed. A third rider, Dr. Samuel Prescott, joined them. All three were stopped by a British patrol, but Prescott escaped and continued warning the countryside with cries of "The British are coming. The redcoats are coming."

Paul Revere was one of the most visible and active Patriots in the time leading up to the Revolutionary War. He won the trust and admiration of men like Samuel Adams, John Hancock, and John Adams. Although he was a hero of the Revolutionary War, Revere always thought of himself as a silversmith. One of his projects, the Liberty Bowl, became a famous commemoration of the rebellion.

Samuel Adams was fifty-eight years old when the British surrendered at Yorktown. He had already outlived many friends, while others retired from politics once their dreams of an independent country had been realized. Adams went on to serve as a state senator, lieutenant governor, and governor of Massachusetts.

CHAPTER 5

Father of the Revolution

When the British surrendered at Yorktown in 1781, a new country, the United States of America, was born. Samuel Adams's objectives had been achieved. At fifty-eight years old, he was ready to spend time with his family. When he arrived home from the Continental Congress, it was to his father-in-law's house in Cambridge. British soldiers had briefly lived in the house on Purchase Street before wrecking it. Money had always been tight for Samuel Adams's family, and it probably worsened during the six years he had been gone. The Adamses often depended on the kindness of family and friends.

In appreciation of Adams's work, the Massachusetts legislature rented the former home of a British official to the Adamses. The family had eagerly been awaiting Samuel's return—Hannah, in particular. Samuel's daughter was now twenty-five, past the age that many women married. She was waiting to have her father's presence at her wedding. Soon after his return, Hannah married Thomas Wells, the younger brother of her stepmother.

To Samuel Adams's delight, his son came home from the war alive. Unfortunately, he had contracted tuberculosis, a contagious and life-threatening disease, and wouldn't be able to practice as a doctor again.

Adams's cousin, John Adams, was selected as U.S. Minister to the British court before being elected to the vice presidency in 1789. The first governor of the state of Massachusetts under the United States of America was none other than John Hancock. Samuel Adams was nominated for secretary of Massachusetts, but lost the election to John Avery. Although wife Betsy was unhappy about the defeat, Adams was relieved. He had lost other elections in his home state and would lose more. Some believed he lost because of his advanced age. Another factor may have been an ongoing feud with the popular John Hancock. During the difficulties of war, Adams thought his wealthy friend didn't do enough to help.

Many people were not as eager for him to leave politics as he was. Friends and admirers, including Thomas Jefferson, called Samuel Adams the Father of the Revolution. After losing the election for secretary of Massachusetts, Adams was nominated for the state senate and won. He still had his causes. One was public education. He also wanted to end slavery throughout the new country. In the 1760s, Betsy Adams had received a female African-American slave as a gift from a family member. Samuel was emphatic that there would be no slave in his house, so he freed the woman, whose name was Surry. Surry lived with and worked for the Adamses for many, many years and was considered a member of the family. Samuel Adams never forgot to ask about her in his letters home during the Revolution. In 1783, Massachusetts had become the first state to outlaw the practice of slavery. Now Adams hoped that other states would follow.

Meanwhile things were heating up with the new government. Hundreds of soldiers were owed back pay, money that the new government lacked. When the soldiers protested at Philadelphia's Independence Hall, they broke windows. The capital was moved to Princeton, New Jersey, and later to Annapolis, Maryland. Massachusetts farmers revolted in another uprising known as Shays' Rebellion. After the war, severe economic problems left Western Massachusetts farmers unable to pay their debts. Part of the problem was that Boston merchants demanded hard currency to pay foreign creditors. They first petitioned the government for paper money, lower taxes, and court reform without success. Led by Captain Daniel Shays, a soldier in the American Revolution and a

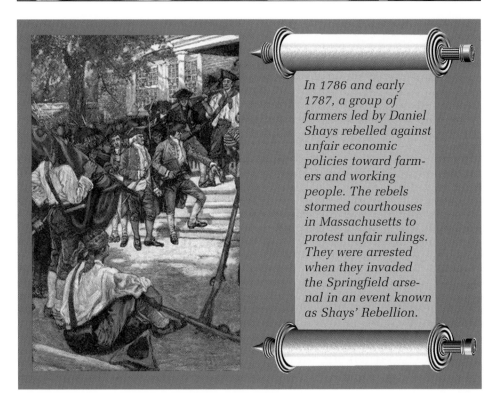

In 1786 and early 1787, a group of farmers led by Daniel Shays rebelled against unfair economic policies toward farmers and working people. The rebels stormed courthouses in Massachusetts to protest unfair rulings. They were arrested when they invaded the Springfield arsenal in an event known as Shays' Rebellion.

farmer from Pelham, the farmers responded with an armed uprising that lasted for six months. The Supreme Judicial Court sentenced fourteen of the rebellion's leaders, including Shays, to death for treason. They were later pardoned by Governor John Hancock. Shays' Rebellion forced people to look at the need for a stronger federal government. Adams was doubtful. He felt that a strong central government would take power away from the states. However, events like Shays' Rebellion indicated that some changes needed to be made. Adams proposed revising the Articles of Confederation; others believed a new set of laws should be made.

A convention met at Philadelphia's Independence Hall on May 25, 1787, with the purpose of reorganizing the federal government. Because of his doubts, Adams did not attend, nor did Patriot Patrick Henry, who believed like Adams that a stronger federal government could be dangerous.

The convention created new guidelines, which the delegates called the U.S. Constitution. After working on it for four months,

the delegates returned to their home states to present the new Constitution. Each state was to approve or reject it. The people were divided, and arguments followed. Federalists supported the Constitution; anti-Federalists did not.

Richard Henry Lee despaired at the lack of provisions to protect "those essential rights of mankind without which liberty cannot exist."[1] Patrick Henry agreed, and the need for a bill of rights became the cry of many anti-Federalists.

Delaware became the first state to ratify the Constitution, followed by Pennsylvania, New Jersey, Georgia, and Connecticut. Originally, the delegates discussed having the usual two-thirds majority (nine states) to pass a new Constitution. Yet they soon decided that all states must ratify it for it to truly be the Constitution of the entire United States. Massachusetts was scheduled to discuss the document in Boston during January 1788. Both Samuel Adams and John Hancock attended as delegates. Adams was debating the Constitution when news from home reached him.

In 1784, the Adams family moved into their own home, a yellow house next to a bakery, on Winter Street. Many thought the house looked the very worn, but Adams found it comfortable. His son lived with him and Betsy because of his illness. He became progressively worse. He died on January 17, 1788, with his father at his bedside. The convention recessed out of respect for Samuel Adams.

When the Massachusetts Constitutional Convention resumed after the funeral of Adams's son, it appeared that Adams might have had a change of heart about the new Constitution. Paul Revere might have had a hand in changing the senator's mind. The silversmith had always had honest dealings with Adams. Revere told Adams that the working men of Boston had gathered at the Green Dragon Tavern and voiced their support for the Constitution. Revere knew Adams had great respect for the working people of Boston.

In *Paul Revere's Ride,* author Fischer writes, "[Revere] was appalled by the disorders of the postwar period and threw his influence behind the framing of a Federal Constitution. When John Hancock and Samuel Adams were reluctant to support its ratification, Paul Revere organized the Boston mechanics into a powerful political force, worked behind the scenes with such effect that is

Written in 1787, the Constitution is the highest law in the United States. It mandates how the government works. All thirteen states ratified the Constitution. Within a few years, the Bill of Rights was added.

commonly thought to have turned the narrow balance in a critical state."[2]

The other delegate, Governor John Hancock, missed the beginning debates due to illness. Pro-Constitution forces visited him also and convinced him that supporting the Constitution was the right thing to do. The federal government needed more power to be effective. Adams and Hancock began talking again. They met at Hancock's home to discuss this new Constitution, and both agreed to support it.

When the Convention came to order on the last day of January in 1788, Hancock gave a speech asking for everyone's support in adopting the Constitution. Once Adams decided to support the document, he did everything he could to help. He convinced indecisive

delegates to support the new federal government. By a margin of nineteen votes, Massachusetts voted to adopt the Constitution. Other colonies had been watching to see what Massachusetts, the leader in the Revolutionary War, would do. Soon Maryland and South Carolina voted to approve it. Within two years, all thirteen colonies ratified the Constitution of the United States.

Adams remained active in protecting the Constitution. He knew it wasn't a perfect document, but he tried to make it so. He and others, like Patrick Henry, sought to make changes to improve it. These changes became the ten amendments, known as the Bill of Rights, which were ratified in December 1791. The Bill of Rights promised people fundamental liberties, including freedom of speech and religion. Today, the Bill of Rights is considered one of the most important parts of the Constitution, and has served as the model for bills of rights in other countries.

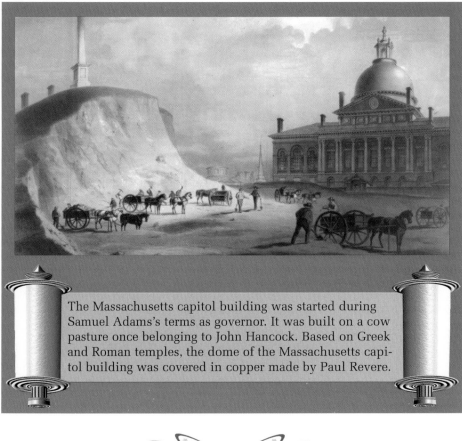

The Massachusetts capitol building was started during Samuel Adams's terms as governor. It was built on a cow pasture once belonging to John Hancock. Based on Greek and Roman temples, the dome of the Massachusetts capitol building was covered in copper made by Paul Revere.

The success of Adams and Hancock at the Massachusetts Constitutional Convention convinced the men to run together for the gubernatorial race. They ran in 1789 and won. John Hancock was again elected governor, with Samuel Adams as lieutenant governor. Both men were advanced in age, Adams more so than Hancock. Adams had uncontrollable shaking that kept him from writing. He often had others, even his grandchildren, do his writing for him.

Hancock's health also continued to deteriorate. He had a disease called gout which led to swelling of the joints. The disease weakened him, and the pain prevented him from walking. In 1793, he died from complications of gout. Adams led the procession for John Hancock's funeral, attended by thousands. Because of his own ill health or because he was overcome with emotion, Adams was not able to make it all the way to the cemetery.

Adams was now governor of Massachusetts. He not only finished Hancock's term, but was elected three more times in the annual elections. As governor, one of his most important objectives was protecting peoples' rights. Still governor at age seventy-four, Samuel Adams holds the record for the oldest governor in Massachusetts history. Adams decided he was done with politics once and for all in 1797 and spent his remaining years with his wife, daughter, three grandchildren, and many friends. He enjoyed recounting to eager listeners the days before the American Revolution. He rejoiced in 1800 when his old friend and Patriot, Thomas Jefferson, was elected the third president of the United States.

Soon after his eighty-first birthday, Samuel Adams died. He would be interred in the Granary Burial Ground, the same place as his friend John Hancock. He had asked that his funeral be the way he liked to live—simple. Yet people poured into the streets and gave speeches about a man to whom they owed so much.

Samuel Adams is a man whose name sometimes gets lost among so many people who fought for American independence. Indeed, Adams never wanted attention for himself. He didn't speak up to gain fame and glory. He only wanted what was best for his country—America. Possibly the nation's first politician, Samuel Adams was a man who started with a seed of an idea—independence—and helped it grow.

John Adams

John Adams (1735–1826) became the first vice president and the second president of the United States. A Massachusetts lawyer, he was probably introduced to the colonial fight for independence by his cousin Samuel.

During the Second Continental Congress, John Adams wrote down his ideas about forming a constitution. These ideas became an essay called *Thoughts on Government*. Richard

John Adams

Henry Lee of Virginia had it printed as a pamphlet, and it was widely distributed. Adams used it himself in 1779 when writing the Massachusetts Constitution, the oldest constitution in the Western world.

As a member of the Continental Congress that drafted the Declaration of Independence, Adams was one of the signers of the very important document. After the Revolutionary War, he became the first vice president, under George Washington. He became the second president in 1796. Adams was the first president to live in the White House when the United States government moved from Philadelphia to Washington, D.C. Industrialization also started during Adams's term. The first woolen mills began operating in Massachusetts. Thanks to Ben Franklin, the Department of the Navy and the Marine Corps were also established at this time. Adams saw a split in his own party when he stayed neutral during the French Revolution. People heard of American ships being attacked and felt that America should go to war against France. Many believe that Adams lost the next election because he kept the peace when so many wanted to go to war. John Adams last served in public office as a member of the Massachusetts Constitutional Convention in 1820.

John Adams was the first president whose son also served as president. John Quincy Adams, also an attorney, served as the sixth president. John Adams died on July 4, 1826, on the same day as Thomas Jefferson. This was, incidentally, the fiftieth anniversary of the signing of the Declaration of Independence.

Chapter Notes

Chapter 1: A Tea Party

1. John K. Alexander, *Samuel Adams: America's Revolutionary Politician* (Lanham, Maryland: Rowman & Littlefield Publishers, Inc., 2002), p. 123.

2. Ibid., pp. 120–121.

3. Ibid., p. 125.

4. Ibid., p. 124.

Chapter 2: Politics

1. David Hackett Fischer, *Paul Revere's Ride* (New York: Oxford University Press, 1994) p. 10.

2. Gordon S. Wood, *The Creation of the American Republic, 1776–1787* (Chapel Hill: University of North Carolina, 1969), p. 151.

3. John K. Alexander, *Samuel Adams: America's Revolutionary Politician* (Lanham, Maryland: Rowman & Littlefield Publishers, Inc., 2002), p. 8.

4. Ibid., p. 9.

5. Ibid., p. 14.

Chapter 3: "Liberty, Property, and No Stamps!"

1. John K. Alexander, *Samuel Adams: America's Revolutionary Politician* (Lanham, Maryland: Rowman & Littlefield Publishers, Inc., 2002), p. 32.

2. Ibid., p. 126.

3. Independence Hall Organization http://www.ushistory.org/declaration/signers/hancock.htm

Chapter 4: The Continental Congress

1. David Hackett Fischer, *Liberty and Freedom* (New York: Oxford University Press, 2005), p. 146.

2. Ibid., pp. 56–57.

3. John K. Alexander, *Samuel Adams: America's Revolutionary Politician* (Lanham, Maryland: Rowman & Littlefield Publishers, Inc., 2002), p. 147.

4. Massachusetts Historical Society, "A Letter from Col. Paul Revere to the Corresponding Secretary [Jeremy Belknap]," 1798, http://www.masshist.org/cabinet/april2002/reveretranscription.htm

Chapter 5: Father of the Revolution

1. U.S. National Archives and Records Administration, "Constitution of the United States" http://www.archives.gov/national-archives-experience/charters/constitution_history.html

2. David Hackett Fischer, *Paul Revere's Ride* (New York: Oxford University Press, 1994), p. 292.

Chronology

1722	Samuel Adams is born on September 27 in Boston, Massachusetts
1743	Earn master's degree from Harvard
1748	Father dies
1749	Mother dies; marries Elizabeth Checkley on October 17
1756	Begins to work as property tax collector
1757	Wife dies
1764	Marries Elizabeth "Betsy" Wells on December 6
1765	Writes a protest to the Stamp Act; helps organize Sons of Liberty; attend Sons of Liberty's first protest August 14; is elected to Massachusetts House of Representatives
1767	Helps organize nonimportation agreement to address the Townshend Acts; drafts Circular Letter to the other colonies
1773	May have signaled the Sons of Liberty to begin the Boston Tea Party on December 16
1774	Organizes distribution of smuggled food donations to besieged Bostonians, attends First Continental Congress
1775	British offer a reward for his (and other Patriot leaders') arrest; escapes Lexington with John Hancock on April 19, just before the battle there begins; attends Second Continental Congress
1776	Signs Declaration of Independence; attends Third Continental Congress
1779	Helps draft Massachusetts State Constitution
1781	Is chosen as president of Massachusetts State Senate
1787	Declines to attend the national Constitutional Convention
1788	His son, Dr. Samuel Adams, dies of tuberculosis on January 17
1789	Is elected lieutenant governor of Massachusetts
1793	Becomes governor on John Hancock's death
1794	Is elected governor; serves until 1797
1803	Dies on October 2; is interred at Granary Burial Ground

Timeline in History

1630	Boston is founded.
1754	French and Indian War begins in the colonies.
1760	George III becomes King of England.
1769	Daniel Boone explores a route to Kentucky through the Cumberland Gap.
1774	First Continental Congress meets on September 5.
1775	Revolutionary War begins on April 19 in Lexington, Massachusetts.
1776	Declaration of Independence is adopted on July 4.
1789	With the ratification of the U.S. Constitution, George Washington becomes the first President of the United States.
1789	French Revolution begins.
1792	New York Stock Exchange is founded.
1792–1815	Napoleonic wars are waged.
1796	John Adams is elected president.
1800	Thomas Jefferson is elected president.
1803	The United States acquires Louisiana Purchase from the French.
1804	Lewis and Clark expedition to explore the West starts May 14.
1812	War of 1812 between U.S. and Britain begins; it ends two years later.
1814	First steam locomotive is designed by George Stephenson.
1830	Andrew Jackson's Indian Removal Act is passed; over 46,000 Native Americans are forced to move west from their homes in the South.
1861	Abraham Lincoln is elected president; the Civil War begins.

Further Reading

For Young Adults

Burgan, Michael. *Samuel Adams: Patriot and Statesman.* Minneapolis: Compass Point Books, 2005.

Davis, Kate. *Samuel Adams.* San Diego: Blackbirch Press, 2002.

Fradin, Dennis. *Samuel Adams: The Father of American Independence.* New York: Clarion Books, 1998.

Jones, Veda Boyd. *Samuel Adams: Patriot.* Philadelphia: Chelsea House Publishers, 2002.

Works Consulted

Alexander, John K. *Samuel Adams: America's Revolutionary Politician.* Lanham, Maryland: Rowman & Littlefield Publishers, Inc., 2002.

Copeland, David A. *Debating the Issues in Colonial Newspapers.* Westport, Connecticut: Greenwood Press, 2000.

Fischer, David Hackett. *Liberty and Freedom.* New York: Oxford University Press, 2005.

———. *Paul Revere's Ride.* New York: Oxford University Press, 1994.

Fowler, William M., Jr. *Samuel Adams: Radical Puritan.* New York: Addison-Wesley Educational Publishers, Inc., 1997.

Lewis, Paul. *The Grand Incendiary: A Biography of Samuel Adams.* New York: Dial Press, 1973.

Wood, Gordon S. *The Creation of the American Republic, 1776–1787.* Chapel Hill: University of North Carolina, 1969.

On the Internet

Boston National Historical Park
http://www.nps.gov/bost/home.htm

Independence Hall Association, USHistory.org
http://www.ushistory.org/

Massachusetts Historical Society, "A Letter from Col. Paul Revere to the Corresponding Secretary [Jeremy Belknap]," 1798, http://www.masshist.org/cabinet/april2002/reveretranscription.htm

The National Archives, "America's Historical Documents"
http://www.archives.gov/historical-docs/

The National Archives, *Charters of Freedom,* "Bill of Rights"
http://www.archives.gov/national-archives-experience/charters/bill_of_rights.html

The Paul Revere House
http://www.paulreverehouse.org/

PBS: *Liberty! The American Revolution*
http://www.pbs.org/ktca/liberty/

Revere, Paul. Letter to Jeremy Belknap, [1798]. Manuscript Collection, Massachusetts Historical Society
http://www.masshist.org/cabinet/april2002/reveretranscription.htm

The White House: "The Presidents of the United States"
http://www.whitehouse.gov/history/presidents/

Glossary

abolitionist (aa-buh-LIH-shuh-nist)
someone who worked to stop slavery.

boycott (BOY-kot)
to refuse to buy something or to take
part in something as a way of making a
protest.

brewery (BROO-uh-ree)
a place that makes beer.

colonist (KAH-luh-nist)
someone who lives in a newly settled
area.

confiscate (KON-fuh-skayt)
to take something away from someone as
a punishment or because that thing is not
allowed.

deacon (DEE-kun)
a person who helps a minister or
preacher.

disperse (dis-PURS)
to scatter.

effigy (EH-fih-jee)
a sculpture or model of a person.

gallows (GAA-lohz)
a wooden frame used in the past for
hanging criminals.

gout (GOWT)
a disease that causes inflammation of
the joints, especially the toes, knees, and
fingers.

gubernatorial (goo-bur-nuh-TOR-ee-ul)
of a governor or of the office of governor.

instigator (IN-stih-gay-tur)
a person who urges or incites.

massacre (MAA-suh-kur)
the brutal killing of a number of people,
often in battle.

militia (muh-LIH-shuh)
a group of citizens who are trained to
fight but who serve only in times of
emergency.

Puritans (PYUR-ih-tins)
Members of the Protestant religious
group that sailed from England to
Massachusetts Bay Colony in 1630.

ratify (RAA-tih-fie)
to agree to or approve officially.

remonstrate (rih MON strayt)
to express a protest or opposition.

repeal (rih-PEEL)
to do away with something officially,
such as a law.

**revolutionary
(reh-vuh-LOO-shuh-nay-ree)**
a person who fights for change in a sys-
tem of government.

tuberculosis (tuh-bur-kyoo-LOH-sis)
a highly contagious bacterial disease that
usually affects the lungs.

tyranny (TEE-ruh-nee)
the ruling of people in a cruel or unjust
way.

Index